Eccentric Orbits

Suman Sharma

Invincible Publishers

"Do not fear to be eccentric in opinion, for every opinion now accepted was once eccentric."

- Bertrand Russell

First Printing: 2020

ISBN: 978-93-89600-31-5

Invincible Publishers

Registered Address: 201A, SAS Tower, Sector 38, Gurgaon - 122003

Dedicated to

Anupunam, my wife, and

Urva, my daughter,

who were deprived of my love and affection at times but not always, when I eccentrically orbited around my elusive poetic center.

Author's Note....

Eccentric Orbits is a collection of poems that essentially reflect eccentric thoughts and don't follow any particular theme. You may deny it vehemently when somebody brands you as an eccentric. Well, all of us are eccentric to some extent with the degree of eccentricity varying from person to person. Nothing wrong in that. It simply means that you are unconventional, strange, and behave weird at times and you refuse to bend your knees to conventions, rituals, and customs.

My beliefs covered with sticky moss
Stalactites dripping in cavern of mind
Grappling with rhyme and rhythm loss
Crush me with hulk of yesteryears behind
Encouraged, I reincarnate and reinvent my goal
My words of wings dust off and start to flutter
While your love infuses
Prana to my slumbering soul
I fly out of self-made misty cave shutter

Best of the people in history were eccentric.

A great writer, Charles Dickens, acted weird as he ran his comb about hundred times a day, just looking at the mirror. He was very obsessed with the North direction that made him sleep facing North. He often travelled towards North, and even carried a compass to face towards North while writing his novels.

Nicholas Tesla was so terribly insane in his personal life that his life would sound weird for a normal person. He was highly obsessed with the number three and hated almost all the other numbers that were not divisible by three. He was also suffering from mysophobia (fear of germs), and had a belief that he would create a germ-free department. Since he was scared of germs, he believed that there would be a lot of germs on his silverware and glassware, which made him use 18 napkins to clean them up subconsciously.

Even the heavenly bodies follow eccentric orbits, elliptical and not circular to balance out the various complex forces and laws of nature.

Aligned with my nature, an eccentric dream of thirteen moons appearing on the horizon are imaged in the ***Thirteen***.

I had an eccentric dream yesternight
Thirteen full moons arose day sky
Crowded horizon, a scary sight
An omen disguised made me cry

Be Careful of What You Wish For cautions you to be watchful of your eccentric desires and longings.

Here I lie, cramped in folds
No maddening crowds
Eternal absolute peace

Obsession or a phobia of a particular number, as faced by Tesla, is amplified in ***Number Six.***

Six, six, six,
If you have a physical eclipse
There is always a divine fix

Inheritance questions the influence of hereditary factors.

Your protruding belly and square-roundish face,

Snub nose and crooked jagged teeth

Your invincible gaucherie lowering your esteem

Roguish arrogance and hysterical bouts of anger

Introverted nature confining you to a hardened shell

Traumatic emotional journey of a woman is portrayed in ***The Mother***

She finally turned into a black hole

No radiation emitted from her grieving soul

Deadly depression took control

Threw her out with a begging bowl

My mathematical and eccentric mind induced me to pose a riddle in ***Hidden Message.***

Perhaps I entered rotten remarks

Deliberate error

Forgone entity remained mystic and transcendent

Lastly, I could not help but pay my tribute to the greatest scientist, Sir Isaac Newton, in a ballad titled **'Newton'**.

Rolled out the optical advances

Hollow tube telescoped cosmic dances

Roots mathematics solved with passion

To every action, there is a reaction

So, be ready to orbit around my eccentric effort!

Table of Contents

Dark Passions...

A tender caress lest you bleed from scars
For every truth, a bouquet of lies spreads
Transfer of passions in dim lit bars
Rampant shots play dirty tricks in your heads
Hasty rouse will end you in fleecy beds

Don't fall from cliffs in to an abyss of time
Blood thrives till the age old clock begins to chime
Lusty bonds lead you into a thorny prison
If you don't trudge in fleshy slush and slime
You have gotten blissful nuptial mission

* * * * *

Hey Dude...

I implore you sulking dude
Stand up and cry aloud
Remove your obscure hood
See the world really good

Flaunt your moustache and stubble
No castles in air and dream bubble
Bleed your tattoos, snakes and cross
Chin up and be your own boss

Stop bending and kissing your knees
Shake your curls if you please
Get naked beyond your façade of no-tears

Get up and face your subconscious fears
Don't be a salivating Pavlov's dog
Don't light candles to dispel the dense fog
Don't suppress your feminine traits
Don't succumb to peer heavy weights

Tenderness, softness and compassion and synergies
A unification of masculine and feminine energies
Unman yourself and splash in the worldly wave
Be a master of those who made you a tethered slave

Hey grasshopper! Don't jump on pebbles and dimes
I know, you are a GOAT-greatest of all times
Go bananas, goof off and don't get pissed off
Life is a rocking replica of crest and trough

* * * * *

Aha...

Arrows of cupid's rose petals fired from a distance
Aha! So you still fondle me and lift me up!
A finer blush suffuses on my pallid cheeks
Cherished moments swim in my drowsy eyes

My auburn hair waits for your gentle touch
Aha! So you still want to unlock my auburn bun!
Encircle your soothing fingers around my nape
Let me stabilise myself against the wall, lest I fall

Without you, my frail life hangs by a thread
Aha! So you still cannot stop thinking of me!
I know absence makes the heart grow stronger
Fear of spilling over of amorous lava is making me crazy

I want to creep up the wall and run to you
Aha! So you still miss me and love me!
My dove like heart lets out nonstop coo calls
Lyrics of love songs all the time looking for a mate

John William's replica painting spilled the beans
Aha! So that was the life I always wanted!
All those beautiful shades portraying a dreamy state
Are all sketchy and elusive in harsh reality

Under the chandelier of star lights of trust
Eyes gleaming with mutual respect are enough
To capture and sustain the essence of love
No more Aha! What a wonderful idea!

* * * * *

Juggler...

Beware! I am a juggler of digital jungle
Unfolding exotic virtual data bundle
Bits and bytes updating your genetic profile
Deceiving your emotions offline and online

I spin endless balls to match with your fads
In quick succession of images and marketing ads
Likes and dislikes from search engines I integrate
From hidden algorithms, your duplicate I create

I throw sparks of tricky apps
On powder keg of alluring traps
I toss and play with passions you expose
By hooking you to the virtual, my power grows

Though it's a thrilling adventure of a unique kind
You must learn to unplug and unwind
Family, relationships and work need your space
Be aware of physical existence and nature's grace
Look beyond jiggery-pokery of flashing lights
Balance is the key to seek and reach glorious heights

* * * * *

Eccentric Orbits...

Arise, O' my somnolent beloved man of passion
See my crimson gentle face post conjugal bliss
Lava flowing through my veins for a candid confession
Before I tumble and fade in the vast abyss

A swarm of chariots galloping with dust approaching fast
Don't you hear the waspy clamour of a conch blow
Trembling chaotic heart inside my chest at full blast
Break away from lust and get ready to face the foe

I drugged you with the magical Aphrodite potion
Ordered Fauns to steal your helmet and armour
Forgive and forget my act of coerced treason
To hallucinate your sanity and unabated vigour

'War is not my choice,' whispered Venus
I obeyed the dictates of my elders
There will be no space between us
When we unite in the heavenly cellar

Venus can only tame daring Mars
In conjunction or opposition
These are not merely stars
But harmonizing energies in motion

Sandro Botticelli's painting brush flew away
Creating an enigmatic art of seduction
Masculinity and femininity at interplay
To appease the forces of mutual destruction

Fast forward to modern times
Men are from Mars, are they?
Eccentric gender bells stop their chimes
Women are from Venus, are they?

* * * * *

Lights-Camera-Action-Smile-Please...

Sunny skies, gentle breezes
Absolute happiness
Storms, rough winds, hailstorms
Utter desperation

Such is the unpredictability of
Weather and life alike
Yet I smiled for
Life is too short to cry

Miserable day, feeling blue
A dirty parasite crawled
And bombed the clean garden
Of my mind and whispered,

Your protruding belly
Square roundish face
Snub nose and
Crooked jagged teeth

Your invincible gaucherie
Lowering your esteem
Roguish arrogance and
Hysterical bouts of anger

Introverted nature
Confining you to a hardened shell
Your physical, emotional
And mental attributes

All stemmed from inheritance,
Mutated demon asserted
Impulsively I ventured
To connect the dots

Lit holy candles
In shady alcoves
Scattered over quiet
Recesses of conscious core
Summoned all ancestors
From their hibernated state
Lined them all
Hardened criminals

Tied the noose of modernity
Around their necks
Tried vainly to hush
Their holy mantras
That chanted softly
In all my organs

Despite my rude acts and curses
They all smiled, blessed me
And vanished in ether world
My pain and sufferings did not end
But I continued to bring
Smiles on unknown faces

The stubborn mania
To bring a smile
Even on waxed lips
Is what I inherited

* * * * *

If I Were A Butterfly...

If I were a butterfly
I will not spread
Sweet poison of gossip
From one ear to another

If I were a butterfly
I will not hum venomous tunes
Dogmatic seditious songs
Malice performances in public

If I were a butterfly
I will not mutate into rumour
Spreading a wild fire
From one city to another

If I were a butterfly
I will not hover for sinful sojourn
In someone else's lap
To shatter a happy home

If I were a butterfly
I will portray beauty and love
Symbolising freedom from
Invisible mental cages

If I were a butterfly
I will pulsate my gossamer wings
Spread the nectar of goodwill and
Fragrance of universal brotherhood

* * * * *

A Droplet...

Reminisce the night snug
Under the brightly lit stars
Softly you pulled the plug
Touched the infinite mind

I hailed your fragrance
When the night blended into dawn
You retreated to a distance
After ephemeral episode of bliss

Call to mind twisting of knees
Peddling the vessel of life
No longer terrified of aching degrees
I found succour in your warm lap

I have taken off
From my small cubicle
Ascended from life trough
Just mingle into my sentiments

Breathe pure happiness
Do away with angst
Kiss my chest with tenderness
Rest a while while I stroke your hair

Why so much fragrance in the air?
Why so much relief in the blazing sun?
Why a wandering picture evolving bare?
Why a gust is expanding to seduce me?

Scare not from the thunderous clouds dark
All the colours you radiated natural
Body mind strike and let out a spark
Showers of love meteors fall from the sky

Live from moment to moment
Infinite drops burst fireworks unique
Life is a droplet in an ocean open
A droplet is my life form

*****

Ashes of A Love Song...

As I light my cigarette
Pinched in crescents of
My glossy lips
I overhear the last crackles

Picture our sinking dreamboat
Through the plumes of smoke
That sailed us
Through teenage past

Memoirs of mischievous
Childlike frolics
Now play hide and seek
In ringed trails

I wish to scrub
Stains of yesteryear tars
Unclutter the mind
Of nicotine fortified façade

Imprints on my soul
Shall remain smeared
With ashes of your
Hypnotic songs of love

* * * * *

Indelible Kiss...

A leisurely kiss not a blend of carnal lust
Etched deep still rattles my inner crusts
On the fateful day, I fell under the abnormal influence
A weight of betrayal still crushes my conscience

Dazzling sequins muttered 'Yes' in her eyes
Flashed the fire in my feeble mind by surprise
Greeted her lips that quivered but said little
Love crystals oriented and blew a silent whistle

Held her unsteady hands and nuzzled soft
Moments of ecstasy leapt us aloft
Mingled with my breath she wished so

Felt her sensations from head to toe
Bathed in our passion, drenched and not reserved
We hopped with delight that we really deserved
Dipped in her orthodox oil of faith, eternal love did not flow
Tormenting my life, she kept rolling me in a wick of hope

Silhouette of embraced lovers sketched in indelible ink
Thirsty remained we for the nectar that we dare not drink
An elemental eroticism sometimes strikes my inner chords
Lyrical vows I chant for her well-being in the name of Lord

* * * * *

Nascent Love...

An accidental bump into her in dingy spaces
Fleeting glances with hesitant love on our faces
A seed geminated in the fallow fields of my heart
A sprout of desire began its candour start

I nurtured it with fantasy and dreams
Rode the waves in the choppy streams
I breathed in and breathed her out slow
Hopes of blissful union continued to grow

I intersected her on every street and went far ahead
Till I noticed the vermillion on her high forehead
A tsunami wave lashed on the mirror of my mind
Washed away my nascent love of a different kind

* * * * *

Puzzle...

A piece from jigsaw life lop-sided and reflective
Hazier with the time, looking for perspective
Gone are the days of blissful, gyrating swings
When my struggling parents gave me wings

In a nest devoid of armour of materialistic frills
Colouring pebbled path of love, crossed many hills
Now I fly beyond the clouds of illusion, it seems
My jumbled life summons the home of past dreams

Attributing my failure to inadequate childhood inspirations
A debauched life now drugged with carnality and hallucinations
I seem to be overlooking my own imperfect mind blanks
I fumble and fume at deluge of life's unending pranks

My parents now hang in a static frame of muddled ends
When will I realize they were my true guardians and friends?

* * * * *

The Mother...

A painting of mother in grey and black
Glided me to my childhood back
I wish I could peep through a crack
Motherless was I in a tiny shack

Seventh daughter – the curse of fate
My arrival not worth to celebrate
All of them were full of hate
Left my mother utterly desolate

I overheard the gossip of aunts
A picture emerged by chance
A blend of black and white stance
A chess board with static pawns

Rooks, knights, horses and bishop
And the king painfully religious
Treated queen mother malicious
Day and night turned vicious

They found faults in her mundane chores
Ridiculed her, even when outdoor
They judged and misjudged her affairs
She sipped her hibernated tears

She finally turned into a black hole
No radiation emitted from her grieving soul
Deadly depression took control
Threw her out with a begging bowl

I never wept in my life
Even in the moments of strife
The painting's colour struck a knife
Apertures opened and I cried

* * * * *

Stalactites of Beliefs...

My beliefs covered with a sticky moss
Stalactites dripping in the cavern of my mind
Grappling with rhyme and rhythm loss
Crush me with hulk of yesteryears behind

Ghostly images twirl laser like wings on fire
Embossing tattoos of criticism on my lips
I stumble and rise with hope and desire
Your support dispels the hazy eclipse

Encouraged, I reincarnate and reinvent my goal
My words of wings dust off and start to flutter
While your love infuses prana to my slumbering soul
I fly out of self-made misty cave shutter

* * * * *

A Warm Hug...

I am made of wax
An exposure of warmth
Forces me to melt

There is no wick
Unlike the candle
So, I don't burn

Come and hug me
Dip in my fluid love
I dip in your love

We become candles
Without wicked wicks
Slender and straight

Let our warmth
Merge into each other
Slowly and softly

We become exoteric
A wicked hugger
On shores of love

* * * * *

Confession...

A deep anguish ascends from abyssal dot
Throaty channels mute the hapless figure

A maskless diver panting to the shore
Scrambles and hides behind the conch eye

Thumping waves of tears swirl around
A jagged pearl forms with blisters of pain

Only a nudge of your love can dislodge
The hibernated tear from its cavern

Absolve me of infidelity asinine
Tiny pearl, a confession of repentance

*****

Hidden Message...

I am sorry
To leave abruptly
Do not know the destination

Destiny will unfold
The dusty carpets
I intend to tread alone.

When free of shackles
Worn accidentally
I will return

When?
Where?
How?
I cannot elaborate

Pain is
My Companion now
Should you feel
The urge to meet me

Here is the riddle
?????
All his brilliant works known
But not the last

Perhaps I entered rotten remarks
Deliberate error
Forgone entity remained mystic and transcendent

Sensibly chalk his colour on grave 1607
Firm and fast
Know my coordinates
In a week thence
Goodbye and
Take care!

* * * * *

Around Your Nape...

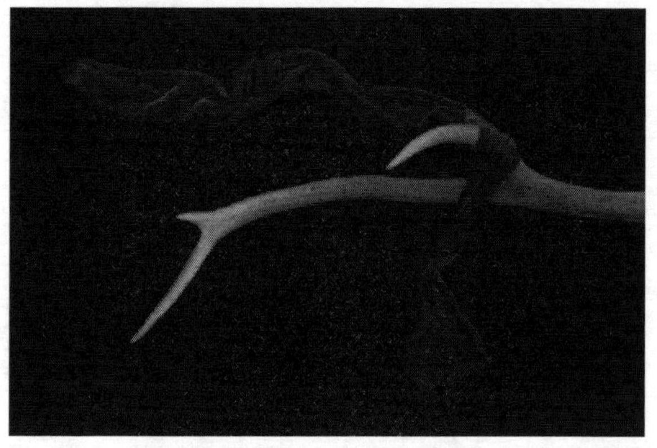

All I have
Memoir of you
Concealed in a closet

A scarf
That flew away
Still flutters

A nostalgic breeze
Galvanises
Wafts of yearning ache

Every day I take out
A shred of thread
From the holy scarf

Tie it to my sacred wrist
And wish for
Our union divine

Some day
Somewhere
In this life

We will roam
With my arms
Around your nape

*****

Bubbles of Tears...

Walled in a soap bubble
I hop on unknown terrains
Sometimes craters of the moon
Where love overflows

At other times
I trudge the mares of Mars
Face red-stained
Spirited but infuriated

Meditated stance
On clouds red
Lightning bolt pierces
My benevolent Thor

I blow rings of melancholy
Eccentric and lame
Stammering I bow to none
But the cawing sounds

The journey is about to end
The bubble is strained
Stretched to limit
Ready to burst

I let the tears flow
Tracks now smooth
Wheels of time
Resonate with my life

Cry
Cry
Cry

At least try it
O Men of pride

*****

Puffy Life...

I am afraid tonight
I might end up fractured
If I take a flight
From the life captured

Words have hurt my ego
Should I hit back
Or behave like a flamingo
Or walk through a crack

Missing a rib of courage
My beak twisted and fragile
Wings of desire rigid mirage
My feet are not agile

May not soar to heights
A spineless dummy sick
Fading distant lights
Flickering frantic wick

Sparkle the smouldering ashes
Pull out the dagger dart
Stitch my bleeding patches
Sing a song to my heart

I look for an asylum
In the folds of nature
Into my subtle silence
When will I be a holy creature?

Love is a hoax
A shaded grey
Life is a cruel joke
An emotional prey

Good or bad
Hide your clocks
Be a person mad
Puff away your smokes

* * * * *

Extroverted Introverted...

Am I an empty shell?
A lonely soul?
As I introspect
I analyse my spectrum
From violet to red
On the life sky of VIBGYOR

My energy level
Resonates with the environment
Loud music
Soft music
All are striking at times

But after a heavy dose
I need to relax
In solitary confinement
I need only
A crumb of the world

I like to be with
Like-minded people
I abhor dual personalities
Half-horse half-man

Few understand
What is going on
In my rotating head
Watching 360 degrees
With aperture open

I work on my own terms
Fully charged or drained
It is my choice
I hibernate
I rise like a Phoenix
From ashes at will

I sing
I dance
I am my master
I am my own slave

I am selective
I choose my circle
I connect with some
I disconnect with others
Only I know
My boundaries

I enjoy
Being unpredictable
Nobody can judge me
Nobody can misjudge me
That is what I am
An extroverted introvert!

* * * * *

Nostalgia...

A boulder
I picked up in
The lanes of youth
Glued to my heart

It burdened me
Time and again
Till
It was unbearable

Little by little
I chiselled it
With my positivity
My smile

It turned out to be
The best masterpiece
In the drawing-room
Of my shabby home

Come soon
Admire and hold
Till I melt
In your arms

* * * * *

My Valentine...

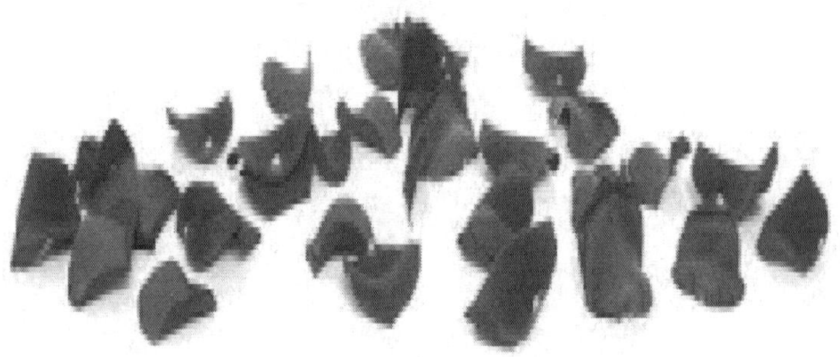

When you passed by me
On a pebbled
Deserted Lovers' lane
You hummed a lyrical song
I was obsessed and intrigued

Next time
You danced
Pebbles flew in the air
Matching your moves
I was obsessed and intrigued

Again, we met
You painted the
Deserted lovers' lane
Vibrant now with hues
I was obsessed and intrigued

On Valentine's day,
I met you again
Hand in hand with my friend
Quaffing and giggling
Lovers' lane littered with rose petals
I was aloof and sad

Year after year
On Valentine's day
I pick a pebble
From lovers' lane
Lob in a nostalgic pond
I am happy and thoughtful

Don't get mesmerised
Rippled images
Juggling pebbles
Tread sensibly
And move on....

* * * * *

Be Careful of What You Wish...

As I came out
Said bye to the tavern
Slurring self-talked
Unsteady gait

Tripped over
A discarded can
Full and unspoiled
Squeaked it strange

A melody flowed
I listened
It sobbed
I consoled

I was intrigued
How can I know?
What is inside?
Nectar or poison?

Should I open it
Or fling it away?
Tried to read
Its ingredients

Brought it
Close to my face
Accidentally kissed
The crumpled can

Popped out the genie
Loud thunderous voice
Asked me
My solitary wish

Perplexed me
I wished for
A peaceful life
Away from madness

Genie rubbed his belly
Said Amen
Pulled me by my hair
And sealed me in the can

Here I lie
cramped in folds
No maddening crowds
Eternal absolute *peace*

Now a transformed genie
I am waiting for a sluggard
To kick me
Out of the can

Be careful
What you wish for

* * * * *

Red Rose of Yesteryear...

An old chandelier faint light twisted
A dilapidated bungalow once existed

Once a witness to chirpy birds
Full of fairies singing merry words

Today waits for heaven in its hell
Wanders in flashback before the farewell

Open my book of memoirs hardened
A red rose lies withered and blackened

* * * * *

Impulse...

Hand in hand
By the fireplace
I stole a kiss
A momentary impulse

Unlocked a door
Wild beast jumped
Irrational flared
Drum echoed

Will there be an end?
Should I dismiss it?

Suspense?
Should I?
Impulsive me
Crossed the fence

* * * * *

Zeroth Law...

There is no point
Looking for crossroads
Where I lost my path
No time travel
Only hazy grey cells

Life was a mess
A splendid open field
A heap of garbage
Beside the bouquet

Troubled waters
Steady currents
Whirl-pooled mind
Waves reined

Coiled serpent-like
Vicious clouds
Soothing rain
Hissing lightening

Signs ignored
Silence guided

Felt like a fish
Out of water
Gasping for breath
Caught the last straw

Don't misunderstand
The heart was not lost
For beautiful rainbow
Or shining full moon

I could not feel
Synchronisation
Brain and heart
At a crucial moment

No remorse
Choices I had enough
Only I peeped into
A wrong window

End justifies the means
End justifies the path
Between birth and death
Infinite curvature and angles

* * * * *

Letter from A daughter...

Solitude I, a teenage daughter, seldom seek
To decrypt riddles of phobias eccentric
Like to experiment for I am not meek
Chemical change brewing up dreams electric

Tantrums I flaunt on trivial issues
Passing through emotional flux magnetic
I cry but need no hypocritical tissues
At times, I feel utterly blue and pathetic

Mood swings lift me to the tree of vicious circles
Where I tend to find solace of lost childhood
My sleep and behaviour patterns roll purple
Twinkling stars in eyes need to be understood

Please be gentle and cope with my aberrations
I assure you my infinite love, my dear parents
Critical phase over, I would meet expectations
Sands of time would mould my hidden talent

* * * * *

Number Six...

Lights
Action
Camera
Click click click
Wait for the trick

Ready for the first shot!

Ascending steps to fort roof
Her sixth toe digit
Mind in doldrums and aloof
Cloven hoof, cloven hoof

Lights
Action
Camera
Click click click
Wait for the trick

Ready for the second shot!

Rising sun casting cupid rays
Seven horses' chariot in gay
She looked at a distance away
Her lover could utter nay
Shiny golden tresses sway

Lights
Action
Camera
Click click click
Wait for the trick

Ready for the third shot!

Both with the naughty beam
Writ large on their faces gleam
Separated by a little stream
Arches carving a novel theme

Lights
Action
Camera
Click click click
Wait for the trick

Ready for the fourth shot!

They pose with eyes locked
At an arm's length blocked
Walking in the air they mocked
Two lovely creatures hopped
Lights
Action
Camera
Click click click
Wait for the trick

Ready for the fifth shot!

Laughing together, so profound
Rolling merrily on the ground
Pigeons fluttering foreground
Hazy mountains in the background.
Lights
Action
Camera
Click click click
Wait for the trick

Ready for the sixth shot!

He is offering water from cupped hands.
A sixth small digit prominently stands
Polydactyl couple destiny expands
They unite with divine commands

Six six six
If you have a physical eclipse
There is always a divine fix

* * * * *

Eddy Currents...

From the pond of clean sentiments still
I drank a cupful of romance at my will
My feeble heart decanted love liquid
To a form with features vivid

As I indulged in daydreaming amorous
Intoxicated I found her glamorous
Lifeforce evaporated bit by bit
I danced with her in nights moonlit

Heart galloped and eyes shone bright
Her invisible strings pulled me tight
Clash of mind and heart she could not guess
Glued lips could not dare to express

Imagined-love chained to my chest
Mind sank in the vortex deepest
I let go illusive burden from my core
I rose to the surface and floated ashore

* * * * *

Crushed Stubs...

Your tacit song on my lips crimson
Puff away smoke in cloudy vision
I inhale your fictional aroma strong
Exhale angst I breathed so long

You stimulated the catalyst in me
Your smoky alluring rings engulfed me
Then you crushed me like a stub
You dirty boots hit me like a club

My curvaceous body and attire silky
Liberated from your clutches filthy
But my mind and spirit are away
Like all those stubs in an ashtray

* * * * *

Labyrinth...

A lonesome stroll in the dimly lit memory lanes
Littered with karmic bundles and deceptive stains
That lay inert and hibernated in dunes of time tyrant
Circumventing carcasses of lusts that remained silent

I pause at the spot where a bright light shone
A hurried glance still blinked there alone
A soft kiss and a warm hug still entwined
Formless lovers' figures lurking behind

Nostalgic feelings make me heave a sigh
Veiled tears trickle from a cloudy sky
I savour the flash of rendezvous ecstatic
Bond was fleeting and breakup dramatic

Don't get lost in a labyrinth of irreversible
Past and future beckoning unknown
Let the life flow like a river and live
But for today with a charming tone

*****

Regal Creation...

Paint my midnight with your mystic quills
Bless me with her meteoric shower thrills
Warm me with cinders of her flame subtle
Drown me in rosy milk of her eyes puddle

Imagine her auburn hair
High bun knotted with care
Sparse eyebrows hide her reaction
Gloss on lips ready for interaction

Lead me to her inner pines
Through pearl dangler chimes
Recolour the hues of her cheeks
Depict what her blush seeks

Smell her aromatic charm
Infuse a dynamic life form
Join me to applaud the regal creation
Give the nascent beauty a standing ovation

* * * * *

Dark Emotions...

Bordering the adolescent age
All eyes did she engage
Glossy lips parted not to speak
But to make a strong heart weak

Eyes glowed on a starry night
Pearl danglers shone bright
A substance of living flesh
Natural and funky fresh

Sombre was her attire
Nobody could umpire

One fine evening of doom
Unknown fruit did she consume

Quenched her virgin thirst
That ascended from her worst

A murky creature arose on its shaky legs
Tongue elongated to lick her fertile eggs
Fangs forked multiple sibilating and sucking
Her pure nectar he found a predator drinking

Craved more and more love potions
Unsatiated remained her dark emotions
Driven into the forest full of lurking beasts
Against the advice of siblings and priests

Deliberately, I padlocked my quivering eyes
Her lapses ignored, silenced secret bell that cries
Before she could elope forever and tear herself apart
With a quill brush, I painted her to my bleeding heart

* * * * *

Acid Lust...

As I stepped into the unfamiliar world
Winds of change my fairy gait unfurled
Boys longing for my glimpse stood entranced
Come Valentine's day, violets dreams danced

I declined love to an overly obsessed lad
A swarm of words flew from honeycomb bad
Threw acid of hate and lustful desire
An organic change brewed up a revolting fire

Dare to relax on pigmented chest and fly to clouds?
Dare to bond with my cracked structural crowds?
Dare to apply a balm of love to an acid scarred mind?
Dare to fade into the horizon leaving past behind?

Look elsewhere, if you crave for skin fair without marks
Or come and embrace me to revel in my inner sparks

* * * * *

Newton...

Born in a dingy hamlet, a tiny tot
Aged three, widowed mother left him to rot
A scarred child, unsocial and aloof
Battled bullies, looked for nature's proof

Yearned secretly to burn his parental shack
Black death altered his destiny track
Opened his inside operating powers
Apple fell to gravity, end of darkest hours

Piercing the celestial reflects
Demystified the law's complex
Light had shown a VIBGYOR vision
Through the intellectual prism

Rolled out the optical advances
Hollow tube telescoped cosmic dances
Roots mathematics solved with passion
To every action, there is a reaction

Planets and comets trajectory
Was his favourite territory
Unveiled the riddled robes of stars
Despite the opponent's constant wars

Tresses of curly hair, he displayed
Lifetime bachelor he remained
Aberration in alchemy flowed
Mercury in his hair glowed

Wished to turn iron to valuable gold
Scanned the Holy Bible for a secret code
As Newton picked up the last pebbles on a seashore
Great sea lay ahead, not discovered before

* * * * *

Dilemma...

There are your shadows all over the walls of yesteryears
Colourful dancing pinching my every open pore
Why do you come back to torment me?
When I am alone in the dark-depressed and tipsy

You left me for sunny pastures of dollar bills
You abused me, programmed me into your web
You, psychic queen, hypnotised me to your dreams
Took me to unknown lands despite my aversion

Your elegance and charm manipulated me, cast a spell dark
You used me, a puppet in your invisible threads
Injected me with animal blood to make me a beast
Cut my all logical parts, made me a dummy figure

I want now to get away, yet cling to the dirty sheets
But cannot separate from her
For she is my shadow divine
My love, my mistress, my nightmare, my abuser

She calls me now and then
I hear her dove call
She is all I have
She is the one I love...

* * * * *

Virtual Daddies...

A rock-hard flower with a wailing core
Ensnared by the dark social media
A fantasy gone haywire in creamy lure
Puffing away anger in whiffed rings

Trampled childhood morphed into hell
Don't squint your eyes to smoky air
Look for the ashes under innocent feet
Save others from the cavalry of virtual daddies

* * * * *

A Forgotten Tale...

Riding on the broomstick of nostalgia
I landed on my hometown shore
Now diffused emptiness prevailed
Muffled voices marinated the ambience

A hint stemmed from eyes frosty
Words drugged with anguish slang
A question posed with littering jumbles
Why did you leave me on dusty rugs?

All my myopic wisdom and black magic
Permutations combinations of allure
Failed to move her satin whiteness
Simply scratched the salty boulders

Now she hangs in my regal mansion
A portrait of love faded and shushed
Alas! I could have shielded the bud
From the intense heat of midnight sun

I wish I could turn back the clock
Mend my impulsive folly and say sorry
There is no time travel in reality
Whispers flow from the waning beauty

* * * * *

Thirteen...

I had an eccentric dream yesternight
Thirteen full moons arose the day sky
Crowded horizon a scary sight
An omen disguised made me cry

I shut the window of my room
Trembling stood I leaned on the wall
Wait for the approaching doom
Some force seemed to call

I remembered all the things I tried
My conducts and ways of past
All life images now amplified
All goods I had amassed

Life, in general, had a meaning
Moved on with trial and error
Gentle was the feeling
Clean was the soul mirror

Encouraged I open the window
All the moons sang hymns
Rising to a harmonious crescendo

* * * * *

Unrequited Love...

Confronting the crushed bouquet of love
Scattered petals of an emotional flower
I lift the cracked lid of my broken heart
That still pines for the vampire queen

Romantic desires sprout wild
Would she allow me to waft off her raw scent?
Would she seduce me with her erotic gestures?
Unrequited love refusing to fade away in the black

My buried adulterated thoughts quivering
In the fantastical maze of lustful desert
Erotic mirages blinking on the cloudy veil
I want to break free but of no avail

Memories of sunny days still haunt me
Need a heavy anaesthetic dose of amnesia
To dissect and operate upon my own heart
Needed a blade of guts, that was missing as usual

Anger, frustration, depression drove me crazy
Till I swallowed another dose of love and cried
Smeared my body with ashes of pain and forgiveness
I am in love with me again, I am whole again

* * * * *

Reveal Thyself...

I have always been branded a sucker atheist
Denouncing rituals of our ancestors and sages
Appeasing stone-hearted occult myriad creatures
Never crossed a shadowy threshold of logical self-cages

Many of us use Gods and emotions as paper napkins
Use and throw in dustbin our forbidden sins and evils
As long as silent holy rites are answered randomly
We are content with our shallow dogmatic opinions

Do we really need the worldly opinion of who we are?
Crafted image status and manipulations on social media?
Projecting what you are not and expecting appreciation
Fluctuating images in shallow waters of world wide web

Go deep, reveal your true self
To those who care for you?
Unmask all superficial facade
And see who notices you?

* * * * *

He Loves Me, He Loves Me Not...

Jumbled by nature
Adorned in pretty flavours
Joy of Creator

Breezy bells jingle
Cosmic dance and bliss tingle
Shy not to mingle

Dew droplets of tears
Thorny pricks of hidden spears
Put behind the fears
Pluck all petals not

He loves me, he loves me not.
Be a happy lot
Let the buds of love blossom
All colours, all shades awesome

* * * * *

A Seeker...

A young monk seeks salvation
Not wandering mind
Dispel primal fears from deep
Alcoves of a dark hub
Absolve me off my carnal sins
Celestial father
Grant me pure serenity
In winter solstice

* * * * *

Mentor...

Yesternight, my dusty books started rumbling
I assumed my matchbox world was crumbling
That contained ossified infinite memoirs matrix
Solving riddles what I gained and what I wasted

An old book, smoky with a tattered cover
Something vague did it try to stutter
All I could listen was a juvenile faint cry
A voice from the past that neither let me live nor die

Time travel back to adolescent donkey's years
Mathematics gripped with hypothetical fears
Uncle John thrashed me mercilessly with a stick
Day and night, he amazed me with many a trick

I despised you for your punishment's sadist
Your romance with maths made you a narcissist
My illiterate submissive mother remained mute
Imagined me to fly high under your parachute

A prisoner of your concepts, numbers, and spaces abstract
I became shy and suppressed my youthful erotic contact
Slogging in theorems, I expanded unconventional
Till I solved the problem of cosmic multi-dimensional

As I approached the podium to dedicate the award
I could not utter your name and role but praised the Lord
Tonight, I realize your fatherly role, dear uncle John
The quest for excellence started by you will carry on

* * * * *

Am I Eccentric?...

The pupils of a normal man
Become twice as large
When he sees
A picture of a nude woman

What happens
When he sees
A nude woman?

Am I normal?
Am I talking sense?
Am I vulgar?

What happens
When I strip off
Show my nude soul

What happens
When I strip off
The scars on my soul

My hopes and fears
Thoughts and dreams
My past and future

Am I Normal?
Am I talking sense?
Am I eccentric?

What happens
When I tear off your mask
Exposing your true nude self

Your perversions
Your deceptions
Your sinful lusts

Are you normal?
Are you in your senses?
Are you eccentric?

The eyes of most hearts
Remain shut on seeing
The soul nude and bare

The soul's beauty
Intensifies
When unadorned

Reveals
True self
Absolute truth

* * * * *

War of Words...

You spit venom
Organs vital hit
Nerves torn apart

I retaliate
Munch your poison
Make it more potent
Toxic of highest order

I spit back
Hissing and mocking
War of words
Blood gushes

Both writhe in pain
Fall exhausted
Bodies charred
Souls die

* * * * *

A Journey...

Billions of atoms and molecules
Create a brilliant grey mass blob
Enclosed by cells, neurons and organs
A human with a pure soul is born

A purposeful journey he begins
Studies and watches his environment
Explores the awesome world
Fascinated by external nurturing

Day dreaming allures him
To leap beyond the boundaries societal
He hops from hope to hope
Moulds himself to insatiable incarnate

Excitement and wonder transports him
To unknown territories of mystic lands
Roller coaster pleasures in full swing
Physical and mental planes get distorted

Embracing attitudes and beliefs of others
A rat race against time continues
He has many things to do
Yet, he has so little time

He forgets and avoids his family
Deprives them of their rightful
Love, care and attention
He judges and misjudges

A strained bond and eerie vacuum
A low self-worth, but a hardened ego
A lurking heath issue, a financial storm
Windows of opportunities shut in dark mind

He blames the administration's social set up,
He blames the politicians, lack of civil amenities,
He blames the lack of civic sense of fellows
He blames the world at large and keeps cribbing.

An unending discontentment spreads its ugly wings
The blob becomes rigid, loses its sheen and its flexibility
It turns inside to find some solace but feels incomplete
It yearns to bond with other blobs of the same frequency
Still panting for excitement, adventure and carnal thrills

An entity emerges and unfolds its magic
This entity is his legend par excellence
Presents the grey masses of past and present
Some reaching to the future, eternity is the limit

The human blob enters the mind of the philosopher
Historians, scientists, poets, and storytellers

Marvels of science and technology are exposed
Coordinates and characters of the universe are traced

And he intends to pass on to future generations
On a reclining, he chills out with a book of
Mark Twain
"Good friends, good books, and a sleepy conscience :
this is the ideal life."
He will leave behind his book,
A legacy of imagined realities

* * * * *

Survivor, Not Victim...

I love my body, curvaceous or out of shape
Washing toxic lust patterns of your dirty mind
Holy rivulet water from the moral landscape
Lonely window in my room needs no blind

A yearlong battle in dingy and sordid blue mind shack
Lying in a foetus position, knees tucked up under the chin
I laboured to absorb the shocks of a brutal attack
White sheets of depression made my world spin

Rising from my own pyre of bluish flames ranting
Sprinkling withered flowers in the innocent soul vase
I will dance in a white flowing frock in a Picasso's painting
And relish my favourite drink by the fireplace

I have the right to wear any outfit, suggestive or skimpy
To gulp down beverages of my choice, hard or soft
Stop treating me as an object of pleasure and wimpy
Blame not the late night bashes that leap me aloft

Dare not to touch me again without my consent
A No means No, whether the gesture be soft or loud
I am a survivor not a victim and will not relent
Till I weed out the sadistic misogynist crowd

* * * * *

Long Time Ago...

It was a long time ago
When I pushed you on a swing

You waited for those magical words
Silent seasons passed in succession
I wish I could have etched on a tree trunk
The four-letter word between I and you

You soared high in the sky
While I remained hesitant
I wish I could have held tight
Your hand, not the moral chains

It was a long time ago
When I crushed my last fling

*****

Hold No Grudges...

Rubbing grey moustaches, curling up the ends
I hurled a WhatsApp message to my childhood self
Let us exchange our seats and make amends
Let us disclose our secrets behind the shelf

Human contact established defying all laws scientific
The gentle soul heard the call from a future unknown
Hid behind his mother on seeing this odd entity terrific
Need time to think, out came the reply in a mild tone

I threw down the gauntlet again through the email
Not to be outdone, the child scribbled on the wall
Throw away your gadgets beside the lonely trail
Get out of your couch if you are ready to play the ball

Open the bundled diaries with sweet and sour verses
Stop making faces at your old self in the mirror of time
Be ready to roam in the nomadic lanes of bliss and curses
Eccentric splashing in the puddles of vibrant prime

Objects in the mirror are closer than they appear
Words etched in the rear-view mirror of your life
Search the alcoves of your inner self, I was always there
Embrace the child in you to dwell in peace and be free of strife

Lesson learnt, aging is a road that all have to tread
Switching roles in time travel is not at all logical
Revel in the moment and mute the clutter inside your head
Life is too short to hold grudges, be practical

*****

Yin and Yang...

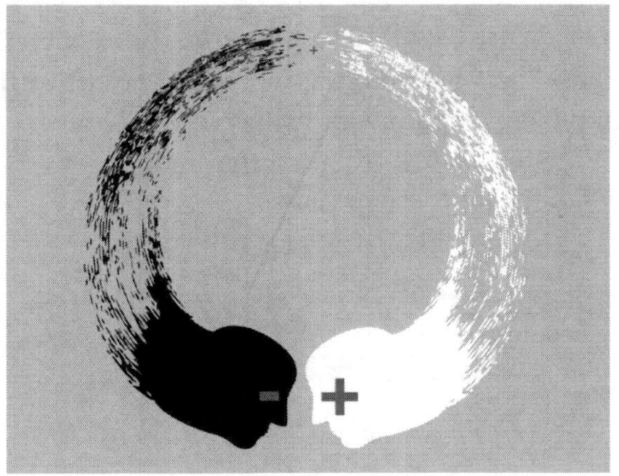

On a high pedestal sits the Goddess in a tranquil pose
An aura of umbra and penumbra engulfs her seat
She spills her royal robe to create a fertile womb
To delve deep into the realms of motherhood divine

Out of clay, she creates a figure unique
Adores it with eyes from the rays of Moon and Sun
Kisses it to implant another eye on its forehead
To attain higher consciousness beyond cosmos

Maternal bliss and sublime love remain elusive for her
More she yearns, further it gallops into the chills of time

Finally embraces the duality, yin and yang, men and women
For the light can only be encountered in the dark tunnels

Humans or animals, all long for what they don't have
Satisfaction, wiser people say, is synonymous to death
As long as you have a desire, you have the instinct to live
But don't flutter like moths towards a paradise of light

White or coloured, all have the same elements of blood
Mind conflicts with matter and good clashes with evil
Live in peace, harmony and all-pervading universal love
Thus, ordained Mother Earth in her silent verses

* * * * *

Wandering Wonder...

I always wondered how my peers
Wandered from one destination to another
Ignoring voices from space between the ears
Chased the mirages devised by some other

I always wondered how my seers
Wandered from one insight to another
Adding exotic anecdotes to induce holy fears
Ignored morals advocated by some other

I always wondered how my teachers
Wandered from one principle to another
Experimenting with fundamental features
Missed the laws invented by some other

I always wondered how my siblings
Wandered from one rivalry to another
Growing together, losing and winning
Lost the chance to understand the other

I always wondered how my better half
Wandered from one pain to another
Silencing her symphonic voice to chaff
Endured and not a word did she utter

I chose to wander on the plane of perceptions
Let everyone to inscribe on my canvas plain
Drenched in downpours of myriad deceptions
Hitchhiked journey points to a destination arcane

* * * * *

Trail of life...

The sky joined me in weeping dry
Tears white flaked balls of cotton
To stuff my ears from hearing
The sound of her departing steps

Footprints of memoirs on the cold canvas
Time will curve inward and dissolve away
The trail will become straight and monotonous
I will snail alone to the finishing line

* * * * *

A Lovelorn Wish...

There are untilled terra firma locations and spots
Interspersed aimlessly among the slushy mind dots
Where you can sow seeds of dahlias and tulips
And nurture with sweet words from your lips
A thousand blooms to entrap your body and mind
I unravel coiled tongues to keep you confined
Convolute you head to toe to creep into voids mystic
You will experience a heavenly dance ballistic

* * * * *

Liquid Desires...

Sometimes grand façades and carnal perceptions
Are drenched in a downpour of ocular deceptions
Illusions induce subtle vibration in our inertial senses
Trigger off desires to jump over moral fences

* * * * *

Hibernated Dreams...

When I am gone forever to the world of ether
Summon up your strength and dig deeper
Open the rusted iron trunk in the basement
Where I stored my diaries of life's statement

You will find these crawling in the dust
Look for the blue diary with a faded crust
Hibernated and curled timidly in a corner
Scribbled wherein are the dreams of a goner

Elusive dreams on the sands of time
Some blossomed into a flower prime
And some withered in the dark stairs

Under the burden of mundane affairs
These dreams sometimes clashed with my soul
And blew the trumpet of war beyond my control
Conflict and dialogue between mind and heart
Pronunciation of verses subtle and minute

At times my dreams providentially won the battle
Another time my soul got engaged in prattle
My life remained as parched as the desert
But mirages did appear but were inert

You are the one to pour a drop of holy water
Read invisible signs in the blank matter
Publish a book of my undreamt vision
Only then will I get ultimate salvation

* * * * *

Puppet...

Ego, the juggler horse with blinkers
Manipulates tricks on beats and wits
Enacts drama with twisted fingers
Duel of logic and feeling it knits
Lesser is the chance to fall in pits
When more is the sync between the two
Fly not the soul from separate cockpits
Unite and dwell only on what is true

* * * * *

Happy and Fulfilled Life...

Bruised mentally by the cactus world hostile
I took a long-overdue break for a while
Wandered alone into a distant fairyland
To wash away dirt from my guilt-ridden hand

By sheer luck, I came across a green shrubbery
Looking at the blue sky lead to no discovery
Deep in the woods stood a smiling tree but battered
Unlike me, a wrinkled bark and few leaves scattered

Asked the tree about the secret to a happy and fulfilled life
The tree advised gracefully to bend even in strife
Encouraged I discussed with the roots, branches and trunks
Shared vagaries of pain and pleasure that came in chunks

All sins photosynthesised into chlorophylls of peace
Optimism flickered and dark phobias tended to cease
As I said goodbye to my immortal friend that still glowed
I bent forward and bowed for the words of wisdom bestowed

* * * * *

Never Ever Look Down on Yourself...

Sailing through the tiny islets of past
I do come across unconscious dreams
Some have morphed into remorse
And some still pining to be fulfilled
I implore them not to fret "if only"

At times I fly into a future unknown
I see Grand Canyons and bright horizons
Some appear to be ostentatious miracles
Others are still in a coarse embryonic stage
I implore not to anticipate "God forbids"

Rendezvous of past and future is a moving dot
Of beginning well as the inevitable end
O' Suman, connect and integrate with present
Leave the clutches of selfish delusions
Egotism, avarice, and perpetual remorse

You are neither the creator nor the destroyer
Do your karma and do not worry about the outcome
That is beyond your natural control
Look back or look forward
But never ever look down on yourself

* * * * *

A Celestial Kiss...

A life of cosy comforts you unwind
With sprigs of mistletoe hanging around
A thousand lives that you ached to find

Try to leave your thorny past behind
A sigh that did not bother to rebound
A life of cosy comforts you unwind

Be cool and heed to your thoughtful mind
Lend your wisdom to inner subtle sound
A thousand lives that you ached to find

Dodge episodes of emotional blind
That cannot find their cordial ground
A life of cosy comforts you unwind

Silent vows chanted in alcoves of mind
Should not be twisted and torn down
A thousand lives that you ached to find

A marital bliss of clouds and sunshine
Even when the world is turned upside down
A life of cosy comforts you unwind
A thousand lives that you ached to find

*****

Better Half...

A pretty reader with a sensitive head
She could not decipher what I said
My poems lacked wit
Random words I knit
To teach me she married me instead

* * * * *

From Dawn to Dusk...

I may not have a sweet aroma
Like roses that everyone loves
I may have yellowed tongued petals
But structured in Fibonacci series

Despite your black spots
That nobody notices
I trust you when you rise
Hug you without shame

From dawn to dusk
I carry your name
And follow you
To my last rites

* * * * *

Aloneness...

A city once my humble home, anonymous now
Littered now with strangers with a frown on the brow

Where do I dump debris of my forlorn love life?
Shredded into pieces by scythe and crooked knife

Whom do I narrate the story of ossified tears?
Who will lend me their patient unflappable ears?

Every night I board the last train to sleepy bed
Shout the story amidst the rattling sounds in my head

Racing dreams and city merge in flirtation
Only to fade in the morning with pangs of separation

* * * * *

Cheers...

I light a candle
Say "Cheers to all"
I blow off my mind
For another sojourn
Of celebration of life

Life is a sum of
Infinitesimal dots of
Happiness and sorrow
Spread randomly

* * * * *

Zig Zag Steps...

Don't
Booze much
Warns my wife
I steal a salivating glance
Colourless liquid beckoning me
To guide me through the stormy life

At last conflict flows out of my mind
Vodka trickles down stomach
Burning the channels
Silence followed
Buds of voice
Sprout

I
Could
Now solve
Complex problems
Chatter non-stop philosophy
Except the solution to my alcoholism

*****

Slanted Stones...

Swallowed by ignorance and hatred
Nostrils spitting fire like dragons
We raise our voice to destruction
To ravage whosoever comes in our way

Peace buried in our own courtyard
Logic thrown into muddy ponds
We continue to chant in freaky bellows
Freedom, justice, and equality

Feet on accelerator of rash spots
With defective brakes of emotions
We found a new weapon
A stone of primitive instincts

A new race has been born
Running helter-skelter
Blind, deaf, and bigoted
With stones to pelt

I keep mum and close my eyes
I cannot see my nation burning
I run back to my cave to hide
And resume my art on stones

* * * * *

Forgive Me Please...

I wish I could now have the nerve to pluck
Dry tears from your blank eyes that get stuck
To implant a kiss on your scarred forehead
And ask for forgiveness for what I said

Allow me to mend the lofty garden trampled
Angry bird game, an innocent prey strangled
As a sadistic fascist confined you to moral chains
While my eccentricity orbits to inflict spooky pains

Indulged in vices, I made you an emotional wreck
Put a garland of bombs and insecurity around your neck
Forced you to become a slave to satiate dark hunger
I slept on cushy beds and confined you to a bunker

Right or wrong, I leave you to decide
I have sinned and admit it from inside
Let go of the past, lend me, my saviour, your gentle hand
Forgiveness, Martin Luther said, is God's command

* * * * *

Circle of Heaven...

A man or a woman per se is a spiritual intellect
Descended in flesh to be absolutely perfect
Got divided in to divine cross of personalities
A swastika whirling around their mentalities

The astral plane of fire is the ego
Where impulse does not let us go
Mental energy is my motif obsessive
I am powerful and possessive

An earthly creature yet headstrong attitude
Material needs fulfilled I simply get along
Bundles of incredible strength I carry
Try not to enter my innermost sanctuary

Intellectual stimulation is what I need
A rational gentleman in word and deed
No airs, but consult me for unbiased advice
Will try to be logical and diplomatically nice

Emotional ripples stream though my psyche
I am so deep a waterbody that you may not like me
Carl Jung or Sigmund Freud may not endorse
We are nascent hierarchies of the divine force

* * * * *

Pen Pointers...

Poets pen poems passionate
Portray possible philosophical pictures
Paint psyche penetrating profound
Possibly put personal perspective

Parables process past personalities
Pastoral ponder perfect peasant
Petrarchan part peculiar package
Precipitated problems pinned

Perhaps purpose promoted partially
Planet peace precipitated perpetual

* * * * *

Distorted Rungs...

To escape the humdrum of life isolated
When his candle was burning halfway
Melted wax hugged with ideas aberrated
Designs never letting him walk away

That night he drank too much
That night he invented too much
That night he reflected too much
Hankered after an elusive touch

A blip of flame escaped on spur of moment
Grasped the ladder of kinky steps in emotive fit

Contacted dark half-moon in unstable movement
To satiate the primal urge devoid of rational wit

Remained suspended inverted in thin air
Infatuated with the gross hypnotic phases
Head hanging in shame and despair
Toes trembling in guilty conscious cages

At last, he cried and saw the remorse
Waiting for admission at his soul's door
Lo! Bright half-moon sloped its course
To kiss the mountains of love, like before

* * * * *

My Poems...

My poems
eccentric puzzles
Random stalactites orbiting in
Cave hidden from curious trippers

Dare to enter?
Switch off your grey cells
Close your mind and follow
Drift of rock smooth heart

Swim in the stream of thoughts
Dive in blue moody echoes
Watchout for for sticky words
And mossed creepy images

I have no dictionary
No sense of grammar
I Grapple with the rhythm
Structureless is my poetic life

If you so desire
Etch some figure
Like a deeper tattoo
Or just put signatures
Of your criticism

If you don't like my poems
I don't care
Just leave my den
Else
I will wreck you
In my poetry
With my invisible pen

* * * * *

About the Author

Alumnus of IIT Delhi and Punjab Engineering College, Chandigarh, Suman Sharma was born and brought up in Punjab (India). Having graduated in Aeronautical Engineering, he had a short stint of teaching undergraduate engineering students at his alma mater in Chandigarh before joining the Government of India and served in various parts of India. He is an avid reader of fiction as well as nonfiction, and his interests include mathematical and predictive astrology.

You may like to visit his poetry blog.:

https://justbenicetoall.blogspot.com
You can drop an email
Sumansharma1960@gmail.com

Another book by Suman Sharma